EVERYDAY MIRACLES

Also by this Author:

Without Apology

MARIE DAERR BOEHRINGER

EVERYDAY
MIRACLES

THE GOLDEN QUILL PRESS
Publishers
Francestown   New Hampshire

Library of Congress Catalog Card Number 83-090322

ISBN 0-8233-0363-2

Printed in the United States of America

To the memory of my mother, who allowed me to ignore more practical pursuits, with the observation, "You're happiest with a pencil in your hand."

ACKNOWLEDGMENTS

Grateful acknowledgment is made to these publications, which first printed some of the contents of this book: *The American Legion Magazine, Christian Herald Magazine, The Christian Home, The Christian Science Monitor, The Denver Post, The Disciple, Gospel Herald, Home Life, Ideals Magazine, IEA News, The Kiwanian, The Lyric, Mature Years, Modern Maturity, New World Outlook, Ohio Motorist Magazine, The Rotarian, Sun Newspapers, Unity,* and *The Wall Street Journal.*

CONTENTS

EVERYDAY MIRACLES

WILD GARDEN

Trilliums born in country wood
Flourish upon this tended lawn,
Finding the shade of maples good,
Liking the feel of city dawn.
Topping the pachysandra beds
And myrtle lighting stars of blue,
They lift their white angelic heads
To catch the changing sidewalk view . . .
Glimpsing sometimes a passerby
Who suddenly sniffs field-black loam,
Sees brick-topped roads and open sky —
And for the moment has come home.

EVERYDAY MIRACLES

How easy it is for us to be
In the midst of a miracle. When you see
The smile of a child — why, you are there.
When the trace of a song hangs on the air
Through a lead-sky day, you can attain
A wealth of wonder. After the rain,
When the earth is washed to a Sunday shine,
You're looking at something that's divine —
And when love pardons the wrongs of the past,
This is a miracle . . . Hold it fast!

COVER

Myrtle is fine for graves. It keeps
Itself neat-combed for him who sleeps
Or him who will not quiet lie,
But must respond to evening sky
And twitch his eyelids when the dawn
Chases the dew beads on the lawn.
It only takes a snip or two
To keep a myrtle plot line-true,
But it is quite another thing
To keep a grave from whispering.

FORECAST

First haze today. A violet blue
Divides the morning world in two.
Still summer-owned, I look ahead
To days when maple trees burn red
And mums as bright as oriole's throat
Will button autumn's overcoat.

15

NO RETURN

I could not find it now — that brook
Which washed chilled clumps of watercress.
Surveyors and bulldozers took
The meadow which the spring would dress
In bluets. Where the cool hushed grove
Sheltered the vireo, there now
Stand condominiums, which drove
Away what neither ax nor plow
Disturbed before. Geraniums grow
In minute beds, and feeders lure
Winter-starved blue jay. Vireo
Does not appear. Except, there were
Notes, one June night, which someone heard . . .
(Nobody saw a small ghost-bird).

CHRISTMAS HOMECOMINGS

All things come home at Christmas . . . Hungry bird
Seeking life-giving suet at the tree
Beside the window. Wanderer strangely spurred
To enter yet again, familiarly,
The door he closed, years back. Small treasures hung
Once more upon the festive glittering bough,
And cherished Christmas carols shyly sung
By smiling children who are learning now
Songs parents long held dear. The kitten found
Lost in the snow, and taken in and fed.
Bright memories that at this time abound
And will not leave. The sweet bells overhead,
Filling the frosty evening with a call
Whose joyous message fast becomes a part
Of us, these holy days . . . and, best of all,
The Christ Child warmly welcomed to our heart.

SOME SPRINGS

I must have seen some springs that did not make
Me catch my breath and wonder, "Is this so —
And can the disappearance of the snow
Have been just yesterday? Did I awake
Today to robin song?" Perhaps this ache
That is half pain, half pleasure, that I know,
Is not an annual thing, and soon will go,
As though it were a sometime sweet mistake
That won't occur again. It may well be
That in some year long gone I did not race
South winds across the meadow, smile to see
First shoot above March ground, first April lace
Of cutleaf maple . . . lift my heart to Thee
In grateful thanks . . . I doubt this was the case.

THIS TIME OF YEAR

This time of year, we all feel kin
To March, whose reputation rests
On slippery walks and gales' wild din,
Who warns birds not to build their nests
Till she is gone — yet on a day
That started bleak, can turn on sun
And make us think that this is May,
And summer's almost here . . . Each one
Of us, I'm sure, can sympathize
With March's blowing hot and cold,
First wrapping earth in icy vise,
Then coaxing out forsythia gold.
She lures us forth with robin's call,
Then orders sleet . . . We run inside . . .
But we forgive her . . . March is all
Our whims and dreams personified.

PERENNIAL NECESSITY

A bedroom window needs a tree —
No matter, size or symmetry —
Just so it has a friendly bough
That on May mornings won't allow
A would-be sleeper to remain
In bed, for rousing bird refrain.
That, when the summer sun is high,
Lifts green umbrellas to the sky,
On autumn days shows red-gold fire
And, through a night of winter ire,
Draws oriental tracery
With branch-strokes black as witchery —
To frame a moon that will not stay,
But goes its restless, silver way.

EVENSONG

Now in the garden, burning bright,
My hyacinths make rainbow light
Where April dusk will soon be night.
With flames of purple, rose and blue,
Their torches form an avenue.
The moth of darkness, passing through,
Is unafraid . . . and, lingering,
He dares to brush gray-powdered wing
Against the fragrant fires of spring.

CONTRAST

For just a minute, yesterday,
I was awake at dawn.
Outside my window, mist and dew
Spilled silver on the lawn.
But when I woke the second time
Bright sunshine washed the air
And dandelions stormed the grass . . .
Rich gold was everywhere.

GREEN APRIL

Winter was sparrow-gray. With eyes not used
To greens I face the backyard lilac tree
And stare at bud-fat branch like one abused
By too much sun. Green strikes a blow at me —
So strong, I find myself subdued and bound
By what had yesterday been charcoal-sketched
Against steel sky. No refuge comes from ground
Across which jade-toned carpets now are stretched,
Nor from a tulip spear, painfully bright,
Piercing not only eyes but captive soul.
No chain could hold me faster than the sight
Of these spring greens which now are making whole
What once in me sustained itself on snow
But now gains nourishment to root and grow.

WEATHER INSURANCE

One sun-splashed May, I finally stood
Beside bluebells in English wood.
A blossoming carpet? Yes, cliché —
And yet it really was that way.
The Labrador loped on ahead.
A pheasant whirred, its wings widespread,
Disturbing ferns that deftly grew
Borders of greens for flowers' blue . . .
And framed for me what would outlast
White-curtained snow, ice-fingered blast.

CHANGE OF CLIMATE

His forecast's "Partly cloudy."
I've found it true, though funny,
That facts don't change, but spirits do,
When he says, "Partly sunny!"

SPRING SONG

All things are now restored. Bird-song gone mute
At autumn's frost, green leaf — a memory
From Aprils past, and fragile fragrant bud
Once more become a sweet reality.
All things are now renewed. Warm rains make clean
The slushy paths, the winter-blackened bough.
What had seemed dark and dead for many months
Has come to life, is filled with promise now.
The human heart can have no other choice
Than to awaken and, like earth, rejoice.

IT'S A SNAP

Now, seasonal as bees and birds,
The shutter-bug invades the scene.
For him we stroll — smell flowers — laugh —
Hold hands — climb stairways — straighten — lean . . .
And squirm at thoughts of winter nights
When we must view us on his screen!

CAPTIVE

The greens of spring won't let me be.
Determined as a vine, they tie
My feet, and I who would be free
From crowded nest and robin's cry,
So I may run to summer's gold,
Can not surrender crocus spear,
And find mysterious tendrils hold
Me April-fast, so I must peer
Entranced again at fragile leaf
That still is baby-velvet, furled
Against the sun, must hold a sheaf
Of tulips close, and trace the curled
Edge of a petal. How can I
Make ready for fall's scarlet fire,
Prepare for winter's black-boughed sky,
Who am green-tangled, and desire
Deep in my heart no other thing
Than to be prisoner of spring?

PETITION

He's sown a dozen packs of seed,
Plied small-size rake and hoe
And asked at least a dozen times,
"When DO you think they'll grow?"
He's sprinkled with such diligence,
The plot is puddle-wet,
And then, exasperated, wailed,
"They haven't come up YET."
He doesn't know I've watched him dig
With Brother's Boy Scout knife
To see if underneath the soil
There might be signs of life.
As horticulturist he fails
But, Lord, don't you agree
He does deserve at least one bloom
For just plain energy?

CITY LILAC

Quite suddenly, first bud was bloom.
An ostentatious purple plume,
Victorian in looks, appeared
One morning after rain had cleared
The sky of doubt. Nodding and fat,
It would have burdened any hat.
The bush nursed droplets, and its scent
Allowed no competition. Bent
On loneliness, the lilac stayed
Thin-branched, and held its meager shade
For one small corner. So aloof,
It scarcely touched the ranch-house roof
And seemed averse to bowing low
To cool the stone-floored patio.
It had position to maintain,
This transplant from a dusty lane
That kept itself cold-leafed and narrow
And harbored only city sparrow.

JUNE GARDEN

Forgive me, Lord, that I forgot
How beautiful Your June could be,
And so must stare in disbelief
At lacy, rustling maple tree;
At velvet rose, whose petals look
So perfect, one must marvel how
They could have sprung from green-sheathed bud;
At bird that teeters on a bough
In glad abandon, and can stir
My heart with song. Forgive me, Lord,
That I leave household tasks undone
For miracles to be explored,
For wonders to be memorized,
Like blossoms, skies and diamond dew . . .

I say, forgive, yet somehow I
Think I'll be smiled upon by You,
Who also chose, that long-gone day,
A garden path — to walk and pray.

PHENOMENON

How strange that I should see the city streets
I walked for years as an uncharted maze,
Yet need no map to run to meadows cloaked
In bluets, reached by green and secret ways
I followed once, can travel easily
To woodland trillium beds whose blooms are pale
As midnight ghosts, and as ephemeral.
May after May, I found them without fail,
And can again . . . I marvel at how fast
My feet, spring-spurred, can reach the gentle past.

APRIL THANKSGIVING

These, too, are times for thanks — these April days
When earth once more shakes off cold sleep, in ways
That can not be ignored — the tulips bold
As banners on parade, the spendthrift gold
Forsythia scatters. Nesting talk of birds,
And winds that give up strident cries for words
No sharper than a whisper. Still-pale shoot
That lifts itself from winter-buried root
And promises a rose will bloom again
In this same spot. The soft warm fall of rain.
Small wonder, hearts, entranced by bud and tree,
Give thanks for spring's invincibility.

TRIUMPH

One sparrow simply won't accept
That spring has come, my feeder's bare.
He wonders if I've overslept.
Is there no breakfast I can share?
Outraged, he hammers at the tray,
As though hard wood could yield some seed.
A lesser bird would fly away,
But he is overcome by greed.
He makes his point. I can't endure
The *rat-tat-tat* of pounding bill.
There must be seed-bits left, I'm sure,
Somewhere. I search the shelf and fill
My hand . . . deliver, smile to see
Him bolt his feast of victory!

SERENITY

All great things happen silently.
When daffodils unfold,
Without a sound dark hills become
Kings' hoards of living gold.

All miracles are quiet-born.
No breath disturbs the tree
That spills from yesterday's dark boughs
This froth-white canopy.

So wonder wakens in the breast.
Serene as birds on wing,
The heart unlocks past seasons' doors
And stirs to meet the spring.

PRE-MORNING MOMENT

It must be captured now, without delay —
This moment when the garden stirs toward light,
Obediently giving up to day
All the soft mysteries of summer night.
The dew will not remain, nor will this coat
Of silver which the zinnia borders wear.
Sleep talk of birds will halt. Instead, each throat
Of still dark-silenced singer will prepare
Its fanfare to the morning just begun.
Fern fronds no longer will be trembling ghosts,
Capitulating gracefully to sun,
They will take shape. Once more, boughs will be hosts
To mist-freed leaves . . . Soon I, slave too of dawn,
Must watch victorious morning cross my lawn.

PUZZLE

If I have not been here before,
Why does the handle of this door
Slip with such ease into my hand?
Why should my feet without command
Walk paths circuitous and dim?
Why should I brush aside a limb
With practiced gesture, knowingly,
Before it ever halted me?
And why can I complete the phrase
A bird starts from the boxwood maze,
Or go unerringly to where
Nicotiana scents the air,
And where, upon a breeze-blessed day,
Petunias dance a slow ballet?
If this to me is untrod sphere,
What is this *Welcome Home* I hear?

CANDLELIGHT SERVICE

We light a candle Christmas Eve
And pass it to another.
It softens faces lined by grief,
It shines on child and mother.
It spills gold light on holly branch
And pine wreaths, scarlet-tied,
On festooned tree that lifts its boughs
In elegance and pride.
Its flame leaps up to each new hand —
A tiny eager sun
That simply can not wait to share
God's news with everyone.

CHRISTMAS EVE CAROL

Hold this night with tenderness —
Candle flame and Star,
Child upon the manger hay,
Where the cattle are.
Angel topping Christmas tree,
Carols in the air,
Snow upon the evening hills,
Quiet as a prayer.
Hold this night with tenderness,
Keep its magic near.
It will live inside your heart
Through the whole new year.

NEW GARDEN

A garden never seen before in spring
Becomes a source of wonder and surprise.
I find that every April day can bring
New evidence of miracles to eyes
That knew another row of hyacinths, but not
This march of color — cream on rose on blue,
That had acquaintance with another plot
Of daffodils, but not this throng that grew
Gold trumpets in such number, that it seems
The sun has left the sky to visit earth.
Spring gardens never known before are dreams
Of bloom to come, and unexpected birth.
My heart gives thanks for violets and knows,
Only a breath away waits summer's rose.

CAN'T BEET IT

My six tomatoes truly made
A tasty appetizer.
(I wish I could forget the bills
For peat and fertilizer).
The carrots which I pulled with pride
Impressed my next-door neighbor.
(My aching spine's a souvenir
Of what they cost in labor).
I will admit the squash I grew
Created a sensation.
(The burn I got while hoeing same
Has healed — with medication).
My garden's been a work of love
And, really, I've adored it.
There's one confession I must make . . .
I simply can't afford it.

AUTUMN ARRIVAL

How quietly the autumn came.
One moment, zinnias on parade
Along the walk. Next, maples flame,
Dahlias bow heads, petunias fade.
One morning, dew is on the rose.
The next, the crimson petals curl
Dark-tinged, and, where the west wind blows,
The ballet-dancer oak leaves whirl.
Entranced, we watched the autumn creep
Into the garden, heard it tell,
All things that grow must also sleep
Until, once more, spring rivers swell . . .
Heard it tell earth it soon will know
The first white whisper of the snow.

VILLAGE SQUARE: JULY

The summer afternoon is bright,
But ghosts are walking, nonetheless,
Along the paths the branches sweep.
Sun touches with a warm caress
The antique cannon's shiny plate
That reads: "To honor those who died,"
And names once shouted here in tag
Blaze with a solemn golden pride.
Wind steps light-footed through the trees
And suddenly I know I hear,
Close to the band-stand's lattice work,
A rallying bugle, sweet and clear.

FRENZIED FORECAST

Our screens were up by the Fourth of July,
So, in line with our usual timing,
I'm betting we'll finish the storm-window chore
As the New Year's bells are chiming.

VICTORY

Now let the autumn have its way.
Hill-smoke, leaf-fire, swallows' flight
And the blue curtaining of day
Against the star-shine of the night.

I who was summer's child and vowed
I could not have enough of gold
And many-shaded green, and cloud
Foaming the skyways, now must hold

This russet glory close to me,
Finding a flaming victory won
By painted branches. Gratefully,
I bask in summer's captured sun.

LEMONADE STAND

Five cents a glass. Small figures wait
Behind the cloth-draped wooden crate.
Patterned by leaves, the sunlight pours
On braids and ruffled pinafores.
I must admit the drink looks thin
(And fingers smudged the glass it's in)
But, Oh, the smiles, the eyes that dance
And will not let my feet advance . . .
Out comes my coin and, cup to lip,
I drink a toast to salesmanship.

PARENTAL PUZZLEMENT

His homework's done to radio,
TV and records' riot . . .
I wonder that his thoughts can flow
In school, where it's so quiet!

SUMMER: SMALL TOWN
(Chagrin Falls, Ohio)

Here is a blend of past and present. Here
Mellow red brick, Victorian gingerbread
And tall, thin windows bring the memories near
On tree-cooled streets. Begonias overhead
In baskets wave fat clusters. Ice cream cones
Tempt the pedestrian, as do the shops
Where one may find a dress in rainbow tones,
Books, handcraft, etchings — and plebian mops,
Or browse among old spoons, cups looking frail
As egg shells, painted with the soft-hued flowers
Of other years . . . Next, lean against the rail
To watch white water give gray rocks a shower.
At dusk, see shadows wrap Triangle Park,
Then wonder which Falls ghosts will stroll the dark.

MORE THAN A SEASON

More than a season, autumn woke
Fires in summer-weary oak,
Gilded the maple leaves like sun,
Told zinnias their work was done.
Spurred monarch butterflies to flight,
Added frost fingers to the night —
Browning the rose that yesterday
Put crimson petals on display.
Prodded the squirrel, carefree still,
To hoarding duties, touched with chill
Wind that only a month before
Sang like springtime's ambassador.
Hastened the travel plans of geese . . .
Readied the earth for snow and peace.

JUNE MIRACLE

The house, unpainted. Broken gate.
Toys, bottles in the yard.
A rambler rose against the porch,
From ground so dry and hard,
One marveled anything could grow.
Red velvet blooms took care
The eye saw nothing but this rose,
And June was everywhere.
Split shutters, rubbish disappeared,
June held the stage . . . I knew,
Neglect by mortals is no match
For what a rose can do!

CONVINCED

I did not see the summer go,
Till it was almost gone,
Till swarms of yellow butterflies
Convened upon my lawn.
I was surprised by burdened boughs,
By thud of crimson fruit,
By warblers which had picked my yard
To map their southward route,
But even then was not convinced
Till from the maple tree
A leaf fell to my outstretched hand . . .
I knew what soon would be.

CONFESSION

I have not wished you back, and yet I find
Myself now fretting that you might not see
This row of early hyacinths, designed
As if for you alone — blue-velvety
And fat, the way you like them. I confess,
I can not feel warm rain on April night
And fail to wonder, "Do you too possess
This blend of pale green things — buds girdled tight
And lacy web of leaves? Can you too know
Mist on your hair, wind on your cheek, or must
You stay oblivious to these, and snow
In meadow ruts, and haze of August dust?"
One fact I see too clearly. With you gone,
Night gives no pillow, and there is no dawn.

AUGUST ASSIGNMENT

I make a closer scrutiny
Of back-yard maple tree today —
So thick with leaves, the sun must flee.
I memorize the velvet way
Roses possess the garden wall,
And listen with attentive ear
To robins' strident pre-rain call . . .
So that, one winter day, I'll hear,
Beyond loud winds and pelting snows,
A bird's clear voice and see, instead
Of drifts and clouds, a yellow rose,
A kindly bower overhead.

BY YOUR LEAF

I'll not pretend my clean lawn's due
To muscle, sweat and labor . . .
Instead, I'll bless the breeze that blew
My leaves straight toward my neighbor!

47

IN CHARGE

Daily from my catalpa tree
The cardinal speaks *Cheer* to me,
Yet keeps his distance prudently.
He looks to me to fill his needs —
My picnic table holds the seeds
On which at dawn and dusk he feeds.
I try to make our friendship grow,
But he's in charge . . . How well I know
Beyond which point I dare not go.

TASTY TRIUMPH

With hoeing, raking, watering
I've toiled — ignoring sun and clock.
Small price to pay! I'm harvesting
The first tomato on the block.

NAP TIME

The Old One nods and closes pale blue eyes.
Doors open to her — stained-glass-windowed, strong,
And she steps into rooms without surprise,
Feeling at home and saying, "I belong
To this." Moss roses stand in bowls. The breeze
Moves curtains of starched lace. The parrot calls,
"Polly wants a cracker," from its stand. Its pleas
Unnoticed, it preens olive wings and falls
Sulkily silent. Music sounds — a tune
That sings of porches, lemonade, the sweet
Nostalgic time of twilight when, too soon,
The darkness walks along the summer street.
The Old One stirs. Reluctantly, at last,
She too strolls earthward from the gentle past.

SEPTEMBER AFTERNOON

In autumn in my lilac tree
Migrating warblers condescend
To toss a jewel tapestry
To leaves mildewed by summer's end.
I must look sharp to see them light.
They are so versed in sleight-of-wing,
I scarce can catch their whirring flight
Behind the foliage curtaining
Their tricks. Baffled by these, I wait
For flash of ruby, glimpse of gold.
A second's pause can mean too late.
A leaf shows gray, the sky is cold . . .
Silence swings on the lilac bough,
Telling me, be content for now.

OLD YEAR'S FAREWELL

I think the Old Year leaves reluctantly.
It gave so much, and found its moments used
In various ways. Perhaps it wept to see
How a spring day was thoughtlessly abused
By one who did not pause for crocus gold
In April lawn, or daffodil's first spear.
Smiled as another watched a rose unfold
And, on an August evening, stopped to hear
Sleep talk of birds. Then, in October's fire,
Sighed over one who had no time to look.
Frowned at those blind to fir tree's snow-draped spire
And to the secrecy of ice-locked brook.
Sometimes I think I heard the Old Year tell
Its young successor, "May they use you well."

FULFILLMENT

Something within me can not be content
With pavements and with buildings, but must find
Itself absorbed in how a reed is bent
By marshes' winds, and how a nest is lined
With skill man can not fathom. Will not let
Me rest until I wade a pasture brook,
Feeling the smooth iced stones, moss-feathers wet
Against my ankles. Something makes me look
At how a bud unlocks its brown-sheathed cage,
How petals form, and how the swallows draw
Sky patterns. Makes me watch as willows rage
Wild-branched in March assaults, and note snow's thaw
In meadow ridge, instead of salted street . . .
Wisely, I yield, and find myself complete.

WINTER WAIT

A tulip bulb beneath the snow
Has crimson-colored plans for spring.
A crocus has no place to go
In winter time, but through the sting
Of icy wind, and under skies
Of sullen lead, it plots the way
To bring a purple-striped surprise
To strollers on a bright March day.
The lilac bough looks brown and dead
Beside the frost-white garden gate,
But quietly it dreams ahead
To fragrant plumes it will create.
The heart, too, has its time to sleep,
Renew itself — and then awake
To hopes that it had buried deep
And fresh, uncharted paths to take.

BEQUEST

These things Grandfather left me — a string bag
Knotted like nets are knotted. "See," he said,
"Properly done, it will not break or sag."
No one had taught him, he just watched . . . A bed
For my best doll. I watched the way his plane
Bit into wood. The shavings fell like curls.
No one had shown him how to use the grain
To best advantage, yet the rings and swirls
Made a design . . . The memory of walks,
Brisk and companionable, small hand held
Firmly by large one, and of backyard talks.
Problems were routed, plans made, fears dispelled.
These are the things Grandfather left . . . I pray
I too may make bequests like these, one day.

DAY IN FEBRUARY

This is a day when white birds fly
Against the leaden vault of sky
And let their feathers fall to earth.
This is a day when leaf's green birth
Seems only dreams . . . The black-lace bough
Is empty of all singing now.
The path, a crooked pencil mark
On paper snow . . . Wood drifts are dark
And tree roots make a cold black knot . . .
And yet, from one small ice-free spot,
The brook lifts its brave voice to sing —
Sealing the certainty of spring.

IT'S SNOW FUN

Some pick secluded slopes to ski
Or coast on roped-off byway . . .
I take my sport conspicuously —
In skids upon the highway.

WHO, ME? I'M FINE

I haven't changed a mite in years —
No bigger and no smaller,
But why must curbs be higher now,
And bus steps, somehow, taller?
My ears and eyes work just as well,
Their power isn't sinking.
The problem? People don't speak up,
And phone-book type is shrinking.
I'm really in great shape these days,
No pesky ills have downed me.
There's nothing wrong with ME, at all . . .
It's just the world around me.

MISNOMER

I say the "common" cold's misnamed.
I must salute its bold defiance.
It seems uncommonly untamed
To sneeze and sniff that way at science.

NINETY-YEAR-OLD

How strange, that verses which she learned in school
Some eighty years ago and never spoke
Since then, can make us look the ignorant fool
When she recites them. Stanzas can evoke
The spartan desk rows and the master who
Relied on birch to prod young memory.
What happened just last night is hazy. Few
Faces are recognized by her. Now she
Whispers instead the names of scholars dead
Long years, or never heard from since the days
They stood before the class and loudly read
Gems from *McGuffey's Reader*, every phrase
Precisely toned. Slaves to her faded eyes,
The past grows vigorous, the present dies.

PROMISE

Some day, perhaps, I may not pause to see
How cardinals sit on bare boughs like fruit,
What tricks are staged by clowning chickadee,
And how the layers of new snowfalls suit
Contours of bird bath, picnic table, post,
Nor how fat buds on lilac branch give lie
To winter's hold, and how all roof tops host
Precisely folded blankets. Perhaps I,
Feeling quite self-sufficient as I go
This white-paved way, will feel no urge to borrow
Serenity from sweep of sky and snow . . .
It will not be today — and not tomorrow.

RESPONSE

There is a look of autumn that I like —
Gold tree against gray cloud, so that the tree
Becomes the sun itself, and all the sky takes on
A light of leaves . . . and smiles back shiningly.

HO HUM

I'll welcome you, seed catalog,
You bright pictorial phony —
From asters straight through zinnias,
Botanical baloney.
Last season, though I spaded deep
And watered, raked and weeded,
The marigolds you promised me
Just never quite succeeded.
The bells of Ireland dangled mute,
The morning glories nodded,
Sweet William wore a sour look,
The pinks would not be prodded . . .
But once again your wiles are strong
And I'm, alas, no wiser,
So send along some liniment
With seeds and fertilizer.

DELIVERY GUARANTEED

Herewith I offer forty whacks,
Or exile to far-distant spots,
To drivers who make high-speed tracks
Of shopping-center parking lots.

DOUBLE TROUBLE

I've learned to face an engine's stall
Without too much dejection —
But must it be at 5 o'clock
And downtown intersection?

CAR-SHOPPER'S GUIDE

What counts? Fast get-away? Control?
Great colors? That's all bunk . . .
With peatmoss, laundry, groceries
To haul, I'd say, "The trunk."

WITH THANKS TO TIME

Each new-found spring, I think again,
It can not be, earth was so green
Last year, after an April rain.
Did tulips really have the sheen
They show me now? I find I look
More closely at the willow tree,
Listen intently to the brook,
View orchards' bridal canopy
With ever-growing thankfulness,
Feel a fresh thrill when house wrens sing.
Then, with a brimming heart, I bless
Awareness only years can bring.

WEATHER-WISE

I don't need radar screens at all.
My forecast's done this way:
Tomorrow rain is sure to fall . . .
I washed the car today.

PILL PROBLEM

"While pushing down, turn," the bottle cap reads.
Toddlers' efforts to open it fizzle . . .
I have the same luck. When it's time for my pill,
I pick up my hammer and chisel.

POSTAL PROTEST

When I'm sending some presents to out-of-town friends,
You'll hear me do plenty of wailing.
My budget was stretched when I purchased the gifts . . .
Then it snaps at the cost of the mailing.

PREVENTIVE MEDICINE

With grunt-inspiring lumbar pain
I pay for gardening binges.
The problem would be solved, it's plain,
If backs just came with hinges.

JUNCOS FEEDING

Juncos show such formality,
I sometimes wonder, do I see
A linen napkin tucked below
Their breast? At first they search the snow,
Then, on staccato wings, explore
The feeder's just-replenished store —
So elegantly that I feel
Honored these guests would take a meal
In our back yard, in company
With sparrow, cardinal, jay — and me.

MANNERLY MEMO

They say, don't argue with a truck.
The best rule: Yield, don't fight . . .
(Now that I drive a mini-car,
Oh, boy, am I polite!)

CLOSING SONG

Who knew you? Not the one who says these words
In a cold parlor heavy with the scent
Of stiff-stemmed tributes. Not this one, but birds
Questioning loudly where the summer went,
And counting on your feeder's riches. These
And the frail winter-battered rose you fed,
Kept mulched and watered till once more the breeze
Of summer touched it. Maples overhead
Aware you watched their march from rosy birth
Through April jades and summer's canopy
Till their capitulation to the earth
In leaf-fall and boughs' final ebony.
Who knew you? Not this one, nor even I —
But blossoms, birds and, now, wild-weeping sky.

ON THE FACE OF IT

In spite of what's said,
I find it surprising
That oi_y to bed
Leads to beauty at rising.

DIARY AUS DEUTSCHLAND

The German Autobahn is great
For speed. You ought to try it.
My question at the "starting gate"
Was: Do I drive or fly it?

PEDESTRIAN VIEWPOINT

I'm most impressed by luxury cars —
Smooth-riding, sweetly humming,
But think jalopies, too, rate stars.
At least, one hears them coming.

IDENTITY

What else could love be but a rose
Which scorns to give itself half-way,
But feels each blood-red petal owes
Its beauty to the summer day?
No bud holds back, no scent is spared.
Each proud leaf-cluster adds its green
To make the bloom with which it's paired
The loveliest thing the eye has seen.
Starting its task at morning's light,
It labors on unstintingly
To reach perfection before night
Shall shade its flawless symmetry.
What else could love be but this flower
That builds from selflessness such power?

ROADSIDE REFLECTION

They tell us Johnny can not read —
And, brother, I believe it.
His problem's DO NOT LITTER signs . . .
To him, they spell out HEAVE IT.

REQUIRED READING

Tailgating — me? Good grief! No way.
This closeness is misleading . . .
I simply am a devotee
Of bumper-sticker reading.

RUSH-HOUR RAMBLINGS

The painting crew has done its job,
The traffic lanes are lined up . . .
The problem it can't lick is those
Who can not make their mind up.

DIETER'S DUE

Oh, calories politely downed
With slimmer friends who dined me,
If you must add an extra pound,
Pray, get thee not behind me.

LIFE STYLES

Some make their lives trim packages —
Well-wrapped, securely tied,
And, having done them up this way,
They view their work with pride.
But some folks tear a little hole,
Expose what others hide —
Then find what neater souls must miss:
Surprises tucked inside!

BRIDGE BUILDER

I find that I can build a bridge,
Although I have no skill
Or knowledge to construct great spans
Across wide waters . . . Still,
I can build bridges linking those
Estranged by word or deed,
Can guide a sympathetic soul
To one who is in need.
In subtle ways I can bring close
Those who were far apart . . .
I can build bridges, not with hands —
But with a loving heart!

STEER STRAIT

I'll wheel my way through thunderstorms
Or fog or flood. I'll gladly face
A hill or hairpin-curve. Then why
Must I succumb to this disgrace?
I'd rather circle 16 blocks
Than back into a parking space.

MOTOR MATTER

Though Junior loves a Sunday ride,
At passing scenes he never looks.
He doesn't give a hoot for hills,
For meadows, horses, trees or brooks . . .
But in the back seat — sprawled, content,
He's catching up on comic books.

EDIBILITY TEST

My pepper plants just don't progress.
My beans seem in a stupor.
To me, my garden looks a mess . . .
The bugs, though, think it's super.

DECISION

This was the spring forsythia did not bloom.
As usual, one wind-engulfed March day,
I cut the boughs which were to light my room,
But only weak green leaves could make their way
From winter sheath. It was the same outside.
While hyacinths rang bells and tulips made
Their march upon the borders, April died
In hedges where forsythia had laid
Its sunny hand before. Ice, I was told,
Played a precisely patterned trick. "But wait,
It will come back next year" . . . I walked where gold
Once showered city corner, garden gate.
In this bomb-periled world, I dared not grieve.
"Next spring" . . . What choice was there but to believe?

COCKTAIL-PARTY PUZZLER

Why do I shout, so I'll be heard
Above all other chatter,
A stream of observations which,
I know, don't really matter?

DIP TRIP

I find a buffet table shows
Affinity for my sleeve . . .
I need a pal to follow close,
Observe — and then retrieve.

MEALTIME MOOCHER

Though he's well stuffed with canine fare,
His brain's alert, designing . . .
Curled underneath his master's chair,
He's whining while we're dining.

MOM'S SEPTEMBER SONG

The beds are made, the dinner planned,
I've swept the kitchen, too,
And now no interruptions mar
That second cup of brew.
The catcher's mitt, the racquet wait,
Without a place to go.
The living room's so still, it seems
You hear the house plants grow.
No cartoons light the TV screen,
No shouts rise from the yard.
The dog looks lost and takes his post
Beside the door, on guard.
All summer long, I've steeled myself
To noises and near-riot,
But now I've met my Waterloo . . .
I just can't bear this quiet!

RENEWAL

How quickly new the mind erases snow.
It only takes a robin in a tree
To occupy the heart with things that grow,
To make the winter melt from memory.
Ice that had locked the earth for barren weeks
Seems but an episode, and substanceless,
When tulip bud, burst from green cloaking, seeks
The sun, and newly wakened maples dress
Themselves in leaves. First wind with velvet tone
Blots out the winter's gales so cleverly,
White drifts are old lost dreams, and spring alone
Becomes at last the one reality.

AWARENESS

Lord, let me love
Each simple thing —
A blossom's petals
Opening;
A butterfly's
Unfolding wing.
The notes a robin
Picks to sing;
Red buds upon
A maple tree;
The fevered search
Of honey bee.
Grant me awareness . . .
Let me see
Wonder in life's
Simplicity.

SNOW-TIME SUCCESS

A catalog-dream garden
Is the happiest kind to plant.
No thrips or aphids in it —
You don't even see an ant.
The tomatoes don't have white-fly,
Worms or any other bugs.
The pole beans climb determinedly,
With no attacks from slugs.
It has beds that need no spading,
Borders never touched by hoe.
Cultivating? Mulching? Raking?
These are chores you'll never know.
Yes, a catalog-dream garden
Is a thing to make one boast . . .
Best of all, it's lush and thriving
At the time you need it most!

A KIND OF MAGIC
(I Remember, I Remember)

I do not know what stands there now.
A condominium perhaps
May have replaced the fields where plow
And harrow did their work, and gaps
Certainly yawn in woods I knew.
There, at cool dusk, the vireo,
Playing a game with shadows, flew
Through green lace boughs, while I, below,
Strained eyes to see, then was content
With just a glimpse of ghostly wing.
I must admit that I lament
Somewhat the changes years must bring —
Yet not entirely. I know
That brooks which yielded watercress
Can chill my hands, like long ago,
And orchard grasses wear a dress
Of bluets, as in days now gone,
While gold and crimson will combine
To fashion that particular dawn
That I considered solely mine . . .
How well I know that memory,
With subtle strength and clever tongue,
Can silence what has come to be —
And keep a child forever young!

THIS HILL

This hill is mine. Although there be
Many to choose from, I can see
I have a kinship with this peak
That climbs as though it, too, would seek
Answers in heaven, yet would stay
In touch with earth's time-tested clay.
Knowing that it would weep to lose
The greens of spring, the maples' hues,
It braves the skies, yet prudently
Keeps toehold on mortality.

ARRIVAL

I hardly saw the spring arrive —
It walked so secretly in shoes
Of velvet leaves, then came alive
In unexpected hillside views
Of daffodils that shouted praise
Through ruffled trumpets, in the pale
Pink-blossom touch of dawn, in rays
Of sun that woke the woodland trail,
Revealing violets that took
Their color from the sky, in fern
That opened plush-soft fronds, in brook
That scattered diamonds in a turn
Through meadow lands, where grasses spread
Their fresh green rugs . . . So quietly
Did spring arrive. No words were said,
Or needed . . . Spring was part of me.

YEAR'S TURN

Old years stay with us. They refuse
To follow any calendar.
Instead, like good old friends, they choose
To hover near us, never far.
Thus we can pick a memory
To chase the darkness from a day,
Or face with brave serenity
New tasks, new crises in a way
The old year taught us. We can call
On skills acquired, virtues learned
In days now past. There is no wall
To shut us off, no bridge is burned
Between the old year and the new . . .
We gather riches from the two.

ENCORE

Most springs I've known refuse to leave my heart.
A daffodil that bloomed one April day,
Gold among greens, simply will not depart
At season's change. It has a baffling way
Of turning up when snow drifts on the sills.
A morning when frost dominates the air
Is certainly no time for daffodils —
And yet I see one blossoming, I swear.
Forsythia is just as obstinate.
Its drama staged in March did not suffice.
Next spring is far too long for it to wait,
And so it picks a day of glittering ice
For its return. Mind says this can not be,
And yet I'm sure I glimpse a bough of gold
Beyond the window's frozen tracery,
Its hundred bells oblivious to cold.
Most springs I've known show neither rhyme nor reason.
Scornful of time, they make their own sweet season.